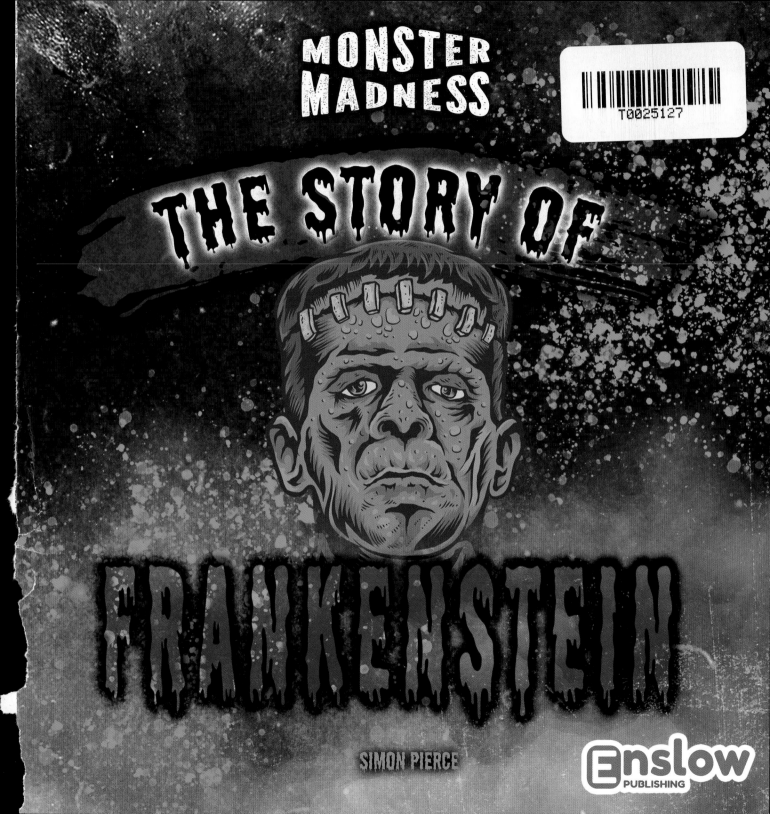

MONSTER MADNESS

THE STORY OF

FRANKENSTEIN

SIMON PIERCE

Enslow PUBLISHING

Please visit our website, www.enslow.com. For a free color catalog of all our high-quality books, call toll free 1-800-398-2504 or fax 1-877-980-4454.

Library of Congress Cataloging-in-Publication Data
Names: Pierce, Simon, author.
Title: The story of Frankenstein / by Simon Pierce.
Description: New York, NY : Gareth Stevens Publishing, [2023] | Series:
    Monster madness | Includes index.
Identifiers: LCCN 2021059967 | ISBN 9781978531703 (library binding) | ISBN
    9781978531680 (paperback) | ISBN 9781978531697 (set) | ISBN
    9781978531710 (ebook)
Subjects: LCSH: Shelley, Mary Wollstonecraft, 1797-1851.
    Frankenstein–Juvenile literature. | Frankenstein's Monster (Fictitious
    character)–Juvenile literature. | Frankenstein films–History and
    criticism–Juvenile literature. | Monsters in literature–Juvenile
    literature.
Classification: LCC PR5397.F73 P54 2023 | DDC 823/.7–dc23/eng/20211209
LC record available at https://lccn.loc.gov/2021059967

Published in 2023 by
Enslow Publishing
29 E. 21st Street
New York, NY 10010

Designer: Tanya Dellaccio
Editor: Jennifer Lombardo

Photo credits: Cover (illustration) haloakuadit/Shutterstock.com; p. 5 (book cover) Claudia Longo/Shutterstock.com; p. 5 (Mary Shelley) https://upload.wikimedia.org/wikipedia/commons/b/b4/Mary_Wollstonecraft_Shelley_Rothwell.tif; p. 7 Ronald Grant Archive/Alamy Images; p. 9 (books) https://upload.wikimedia.org/wikipedia/commons/c/c0/Editions_of_Frankenstein.jpg; p. 9 (Frankenstein's monster) https://upload.wikimedia.org/wikipedia/commons/a/a7/Frankenstein%27s_monster_%28Boris_Karloff%29.jpg; p. 11 imageBROKER.com/Shutterstock.com; p. 13 (illustration) https://upload.wikimedia.org/wikipedia/commons/e/e6/Frontispiece_to_Frankenstein_1831.jpg; p. 13 (movie poster) https://upload.wikimedia.org/wikipedia/commons/9/92/Frankenstein_poster_1931.jpg; p. 15 (background) Johannes Brunner/Shutterstock.com; p. 17 Album/Alamy Images; p. 19 (movie poster) Everett Collection Inc./Alamy Images; p. 19 (cereal box) Sheila Fitzgerald/Shutterstock.com; p. 21 pirke/Shutterstock.com.

CPSIA compliance information: Batch #CSENS23: For further information contact Enslow Publishing, New York, New York, at 1-800-398-2504.

Find us on

CONTENTS

Boldface words appear in the glossary.

AN OLD MONSTER

Frankenstein was written in 1817 by Mary Shelley. She was only 18 years old when she started writing it! One night, Mary was spending time with some friends and her husband, Percy. They decided to have a contest to see who could write the scariest story. *Frankenstein* won the **contest**.

Everyone thought Mary's book was so good that she decided to have it **published**. Readers loved it! Today, more than 200 years later, the book is still popular. There are also a lot of movies based on the book.

MARY SHELLEY TOLD PEOPLE THE IDEA FOR FRANKENSTEIN'S MONSTER CAME TO HER IN A NIGHTMARE.

BELIEVE IT OR NOT!

FRANKENSTEIN IS THE NAME OF THE SCIENTIST IN MARY'S STORY. THE CORRECT NAME FOR THE CREATURE IS FRANKENSTEIN'S MONSTER. HE IS NEVER GIVEN A REAL NAME IN THE BOOK. NO ONE IS SURE WHY PEOPLE STARTED CALLING THE MONSTER FRANKENSTEIN!

INSIDE THE STORY

Frankenstein starts with a man named Robert Walton meeting Victor Frankenstein in the Arctic. Frankenstein tells Walton about how he grew up and went to a **university** to study science. After awhile, he realizes he might have learned enough to create a person.

Frankenstein makes his creature by putting other people's body parts together. He brings the creature to life, but then he is **horrified** with himself for what he's done. Instead of taking care of the creature, he runs away and leaves him on his own.

MOST MOVIES USE LIGHTNING TO BRING THE MONSTER TO LIFE.

PART OF WHAT MIGHT HAVE **INSPIRED** MARY SHELLEY WAS THE WORK SCIENTISTS WERE DOING EVEN BEFORE SHE WROTE HER BOOK. IN 1780, LUIGI GALVANI LEARNED THAT SHOCKING DEAD FROGS' LEGS WITH ELECTRICITY COULD MAKE THEM MOVE LIKE THEY WERE ALIVE.

Two years later, Frankenstein gets a letter from his father. It says his brother, William, has been killed. The family's housekeeper, Justine, is blamed. However, when Frankenstein gets to the house, he sees the monster nearby. He realizes the monster was really the one who killed William.

Frankenstein is scared to tell anyone this because then he would have to tell them he made the monster. Because he doesn't tell the truth, Justine is sentenced to death. Frankenstein feels **responsible** for the deaths of Justine and William.

BELIEVE IT OR NOT!

SCIENCE FICTION, OR SCI-FI, IMAGINES HOW SCIENCE COULD CHANGE THE FUTURE. *FRANKENSTEIN* WAS THE FIRST SCI-FI BOOK EVER WRITTEN! THIS IS WHY MARY SHELLEY IS SOMETIMES CALLED "THE MOTHER OF SCIENCE FICTION." TODAY, SCI-FI IS VERY POPULAR.

FRANKENSTEIN IS SO POPULAR THAT IT HAS BEEN REPUBLISHED MANY TIMES.

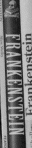

Frankenstein goes to the mountains to feel better. The creature finds him there and asks Frankenstein to make him a wife. Frankenstein says yes and starts to do it, but then he changes his mind. He throws the wife's body parts into the ocean.

The creature is so mad at Frankenstein that he decides to take **revenge**. He kills Frankenstein's best friend. Later, after Frankenstein gets married, the creature also kills his wife. In anger, Frankenstein chases the monster to the Arctic. Frankenstein dies after telling Walton his story.

FRANKENSTEIN AND THE CREATURE MEET ON THIS GLACIER IN FRANCE.

MER DE GLACE GLACIER

A DIFFERENT LOOK

In 1931, Universal Pictures made a movie called *Frankenstein*. It was based on the book, but it changed a lot of things. Some of those things forever changed the way people imagine Frankenstein's monster. For example, in the book, the monster's skin is yellow. However, the movie was filmed in black and white, and yellow didn't show up well.

To fix this problem, Universal made the monster green—and this color stuck! Today, if you see Frankenstein's monster as a picture, a Halloween mask, or a doll, he's almost always green.

THE 1931 MOVIE ALSO SHOWED THE MONSTER WITH A FLAT HEAD, SCARS, AND BOLTS IN ITS NECK. THESE WERE MEANT TO BE THE **ELECTRODES** THAT HELPED BRING IT TO LIFE. HOWEVER, NONE OF THESE THINGS ARE MENTIONED IN THE BOOK.

FRANKENSTEIN

THE MAN WHO MADE A MONSTER

with

COLIN CLIVE, MAE CLARKE, JOHN BOLES, BORIS KARLOFF, DWIGHT FRYE, EDW. VAN SLOAN & FREDERIC KERR

Based upon the Mary Wollstonecraft Shelley Story

Adapted by John L. Balderston from the play by Peggy Webling

DIRECTED BY JAMES WHALE · A UNIVERSAL PICTURE · PRODUCED BY CARL LAEMMLE, JR.

THIS DRAWING FROM THE BOOK SHOWS FRANKENSTEIN (RIGHT) AND THE MONSTER (LEFT).

IT'S ALIVE, IGOR!

In the movie, when the creature comes to life, Frankenstein shouts, "It's alive!" Then there's a crack of thunder. However, this scene wasn't planned that way!

In the 1930s, a group would watch a movie before it came out and decide what to **censor**. After saying "It's alive," Frankenstein says he knows what it feels like to be God. The group thought that would be **offensive** to Christians, so they wanted it taken out. To hide the words, the sound of thunder was added.

BOOK VS. MOVIE

IN THE BOOK...

FRANKENSTEIN TELLS HIS STORY TO WALTON.

FRANKENSTEIN WORKS BY HIMSELF.

THE MONSTER SPEAKS AND READS WELL.

THE CREATION SCENE IS SKIPPED OVER.

FRANKENSTEIN DIES.

THE MONSTER HAS YELLOW SKIN AND LOOKS LIKE A NORMAL PERSON.

THE MONSTER KILLS PEOPLE FOR REVENGE ON FRANKENSTEIN.

FRANKENSTEIN RUNS AWAY FROM HIS CREATURE.

THE SCIENTIST IS NAMED VICTOR FRANKENSTEIN.

IN THE MOVIE...

WALTON ISN'T IN IT.

FRANKENSTEIN HAS A HELPER.

THE MONSTER CAN ONLY MAKE NOISES.

THE CREATION SCENE IS AN IMPORTANT PART.

FRANKENSTEIN LIVES.

THE MONSTER HAS GREEN SKIN, A FLAT HEAD, AND ELECTRODES IN HIS NECK.

THE MONSTER MAINLY KILLS PEOPLE BECAUSE HE'S ANGRY AT THEM FOR TRYING TO HURT HIM.

FRANKENSTEIN TRIES TO KILL HIS CREATURE.

THE SCIENTIST IS NAMED HENRY FRANKENSTEIN.

THERE ARE MANY DIFFERENCES BETWEEN MARY SHELLEY'S BOOK AND THE 1931 *FRANKENSTEIN* MOVIE.

BELIEVE IT OR NOT!

"IT'S ALIVE!" BECAME AN **ICONIC** LINE, AND OTHER MOVIES AND TV SHOWS SOMETIMES USE THE LINE AS A JOKE. WHEN THEY DO, THEY ALMOST ALWAYS FOLLOW IT WITH THE SOUND OF THUNDER. THIS SHOWS HOW POPULAR THE 1931 MOVIE STILL IS.

Another thing that's stuck around in our idea of the story of Frankenstein is Frankenstein's helper. In the 1931 movie, his name is Fritz. He calls Frankenstein "master" and does whatever he's asked. In two movies that followed *Frankenstein*, *Son of Frankenstein* and *The Ghost of Frankenstein*, Frankenstein had a new helper named Ygor. Later, the spelling changed to Igor.

Today, people almost always imagine mad scientists with a helper who acts like Fritz but is named Igor. It's done so often that it's turned into a trope.

BELIEVE IT OR NOT!

A TROPE IS SOMETHING STORYTELLERS USE AS A SORT OF SHORTCUT TO GET AN IDEA ACROSS TO THE PERSON WHO'S READING, WATCHING, OR LISTENING. IGOR AS A MAD SCIENTIST'S HELPER IS SOMETHING ALMOST EVERYBODY KNOWS ABOUT AND RECOGNIZES RIGHT AWAY.

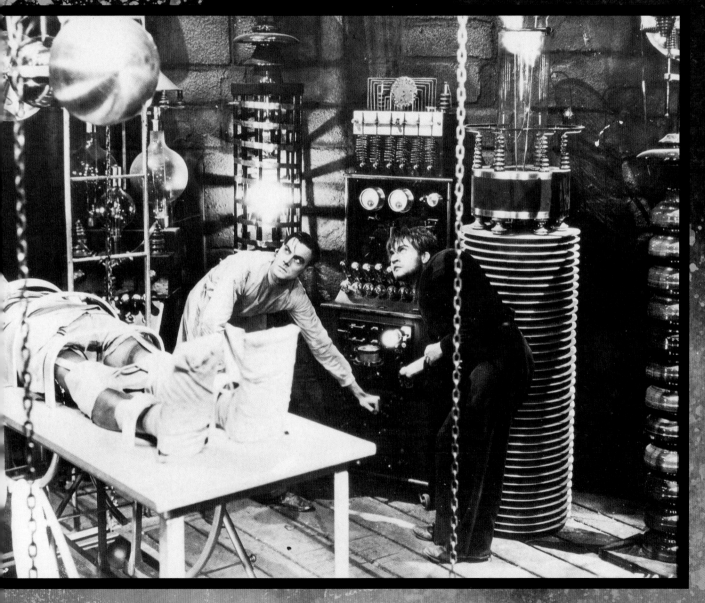

THIS PICTURE FROM THE 1931 MOVIE SHOWS FRANKENSTEIN (LEFT) AND FRITZ (RIGHT).

FUNNY FRANKENSTEINS

Over the years, Frankenstein has sometimes gone from scary to funny. One of the most popular funny Frankenstein movies came out in 1974. It's called *Young Frankenstein*, and it's about Victor's grandson following in his footsteps. The monster he creates turns out to be a great dancer!

Another thing that came out in the 1970s was a cereal called Franken Berry. In the commercials, the monster is sad when kids are scared of him because he just wants to give them his strawberry-flavored cereal. Franken Berry cereal is still sold today!

YOUNG FRANKENSTEIN THE MOVIE WAS TURNED INTO A BROADWAY MUSICAL. IT OPENED IN 2007.

FRANKEN BERRY IS PART OF A GROUP OF MONSTER CEREALS.

BELIEVE IT OR NOT!

SOMETIMES WHEN PEOPLE TALK ABOUT WEIRD MASH-UPS, THEY PUT "FRANKEN" IN FRONT OF ANOTHER WORD. FOR EXAMPLE, IF SOMEONE MADE DINNER WITH ALL THE LEFTOVERS IN THEIR FRIDGE, THEY MIGHT CALL IT A "FRANKENMEAL."

REAL-LIFE SCIENCE

In the 1930s, a Russian scientist wanted to learn how to bring people and animals back to life. He built something he called an autojektor. It pumped blood in and out of the body, acting like the heart. However, the scientist never **reanimated** anyone with this machine.

Years later, doctors made the autojektor better and renamed it the heart-lung machine. It is used today during heart operations. While the heart is stopped, it can't move the blood to keep the body alive. The heart-lung machine does the work for it until the operation is over.

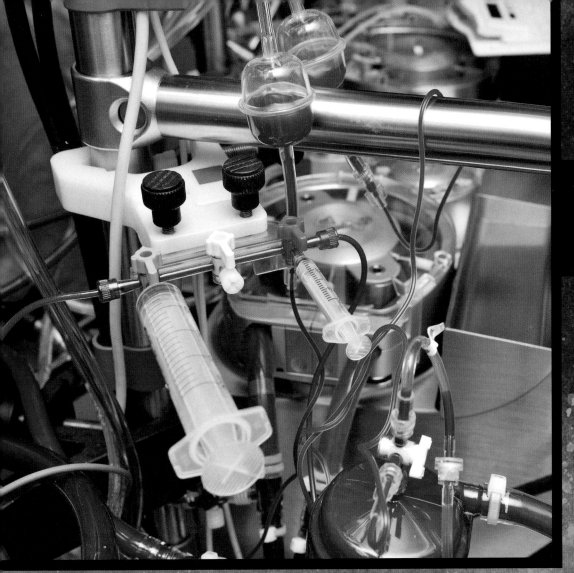

A HEART-LUNG MACHINE WORKS BY MOVING BLOOD THROUGH PLASTIC TUBES.

BELIEVE IT OR NOT!

IN 1931, WHEN A KID NAMED EARL BAKKEN WATCHED *FRANKENSTEIN*, HE WAS INSPIRED BY THE USE OF ELECTRICITY. WHEN HE GREW UP, HE MADE A MACHINE CALLED A PACEMAKER. IT USES ELECTRICITY TO KEEP A PERSON'S HEART BEATING PROPERLY.

GLOSSARY

censor: To take out things that are considered offensive.

contest: An event in which people try to win by doing something better than others.

electrodes: The points at which electricity enters or leaves a circuit.

horrified: Feeling great fear, dread, or shock.

iconic: Widely recognized and liked.

inspire: To cause someone to want to do something.

offensive: Rude or upsetting.

publish: To make written works available for sale.

reanimate: To give new life or energy to something.

responsible: Getting the credit or blame for an action or decision.

revenge: To harm someone in return for harm done.

university: A school for higher learning.

FOR MORE INFORMATION

BOOKS

Abdo, Kenny. *Frankenstein*. Minneapolis, MN: Bolt!, 2019.

Fulton, Lynn, Felicita Sala, and Joanna Daniel. *She Made a Monster: How Mary Shelley Created Frankenstein*. Fairfax, VA: Library Ideas, 2019.

Keenan, Sheila, and David Malan. *What Is the Story of Frankenstein?* New York, NY: Penguin Workshop, 2019.

WEBSITES

Bedtime History: "The History of Mary Shelley and Frankenstein for Kids"
bedtimehistorystories.com/the-history-of-mary-shelley-and-frankenstein-for-kids
Read or listen to this article to learn more about Mary Shelley's life and her famous book.

BrainPOP: Frankenstein
www.brainpop.com/english/famousauthorsandbooks/frankenstein
Watch a short video, take quizzes, and play games to learn more about the book.

INDEX